my friendly neighborhood

Principal

Published in the United States of America by Cherry Lake Publishing
Ann Arbor, Michigan
www.cherrylakepublishing.com

Reading Adviser: Marla Conn MS, Ed., Literacy specialist, Read-Ability, Inc.
Book Design: Jennifer Wahi
Illustrator: Jeff Bane

Photo Credits: © DGLimages / Shutterstock.com, 5, 9; © Stuart Monk / Shutterstock.com, 7; © Ashley LaBonde, Wide Eyed Studios / flickr.com, 11; © Blend Images / Shutterstock.com, 13, 17; © wavebreakmedia / Shutterstock.com, 15; © Tyler Olson / Shutterstock.com, 19; © Monkey Business Images / Shutterstock.com, 21; © GagliardiImages / Shutterstock.com, 23; Cover, 2, 3, 6, 10, 14, 24, Jeff Bane

Copyright ©2018 by Cherry Lake Publishing
All rights reserved. No part of this book may be reproduced or utilized in any form or by any means without written permission from the publisher.

Library of Congress Cataloging-in-Publication Data

Names: Devera, Czeena, author.
Title: Principal / by: Czeena Devera.
Description: Ann Arbor, Michigan : Cherry Lake Publishing, [2018] | Series: My Friendly Neighborhood | Includes index. | Audience: Grades: K to Grade 3.
Identifiers: LCCN 2017030508| ISBN 9781534107182 (hardcover) | ISBN 9781534109162 (pdf) | ISBN 9781534108172 (paperback) | ISBN 9781534120150 (hosted ebook)
Subjects: LCSH: School principals--Juvenile literature. | School management and organization--Juvenile literature.
Classification: LCC LB2831.9 .D48 2018 | DDC 371.2/012--dc23
LC record available at https://lccn.loc.gov/2017030508

Printed in the United States of America
Corporate Graphics

table of contents

Neighborhood Helper 4

Glossary 24

Index 24

About the author: Czeena Devera grew up in the sweltering heat of Arizona surrounded by books, quite literally as her childhood bedroom had built-in bookshelves constantly overflowing. She now lives in Michigan with an even bigger library of books.

About the illustrator: Jeff Bane and his two business partners own a studio along the American River in Folsom, California, home of the 1849 Gold Rush. When Jeff's not sketching or illustrating for clients, he's either swimming or kayaking in the river to relax.

neighborhood helper

Principals are leaders. They are helpers. They are planners. They work with many people.

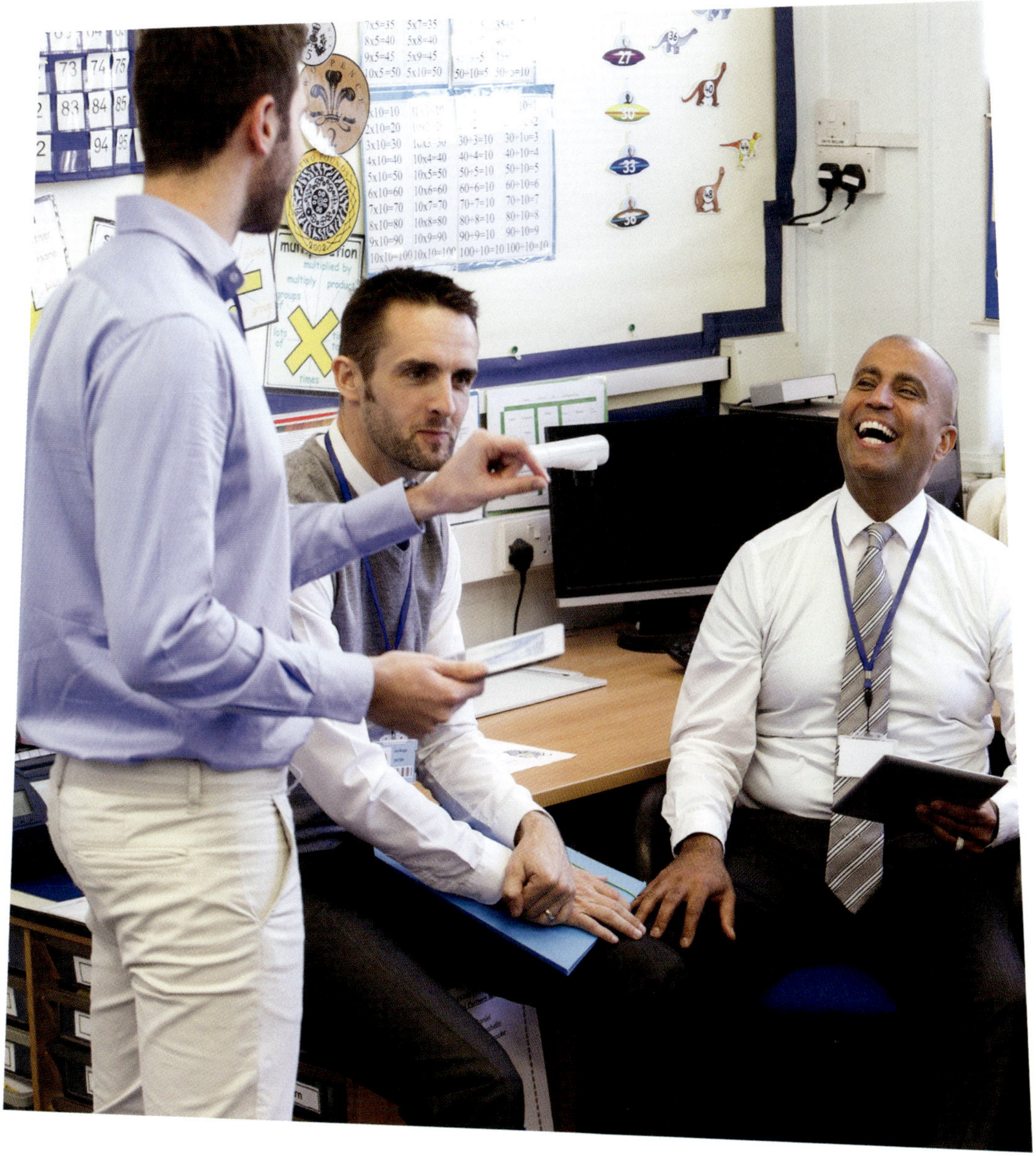
multiplied by
multiply
product
groups
times

Principals lead the school. They work to **improve** it. They help start school clubs. They help start sports teams.

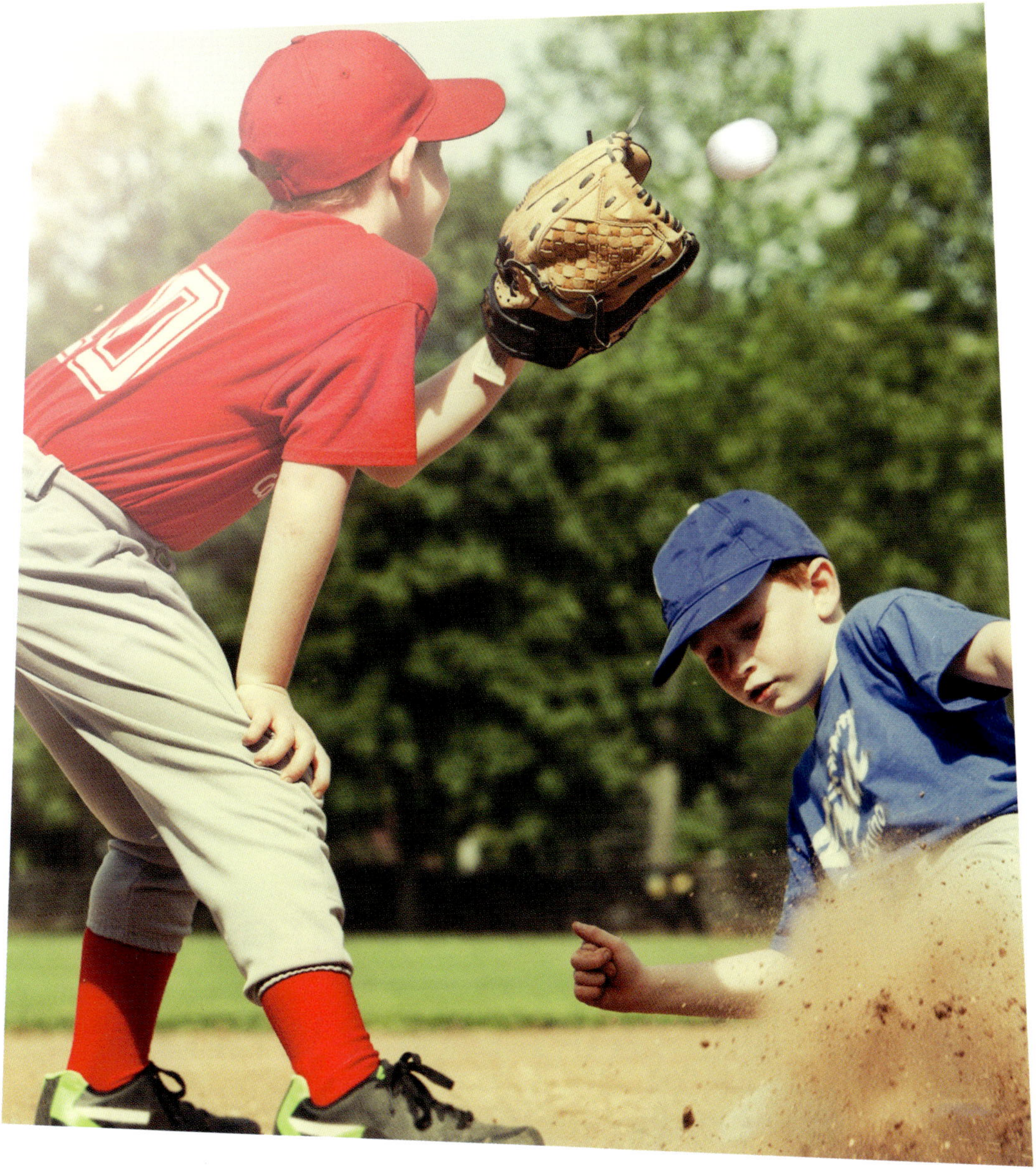

They help students learn new skills. Principals work with teachers to do this.

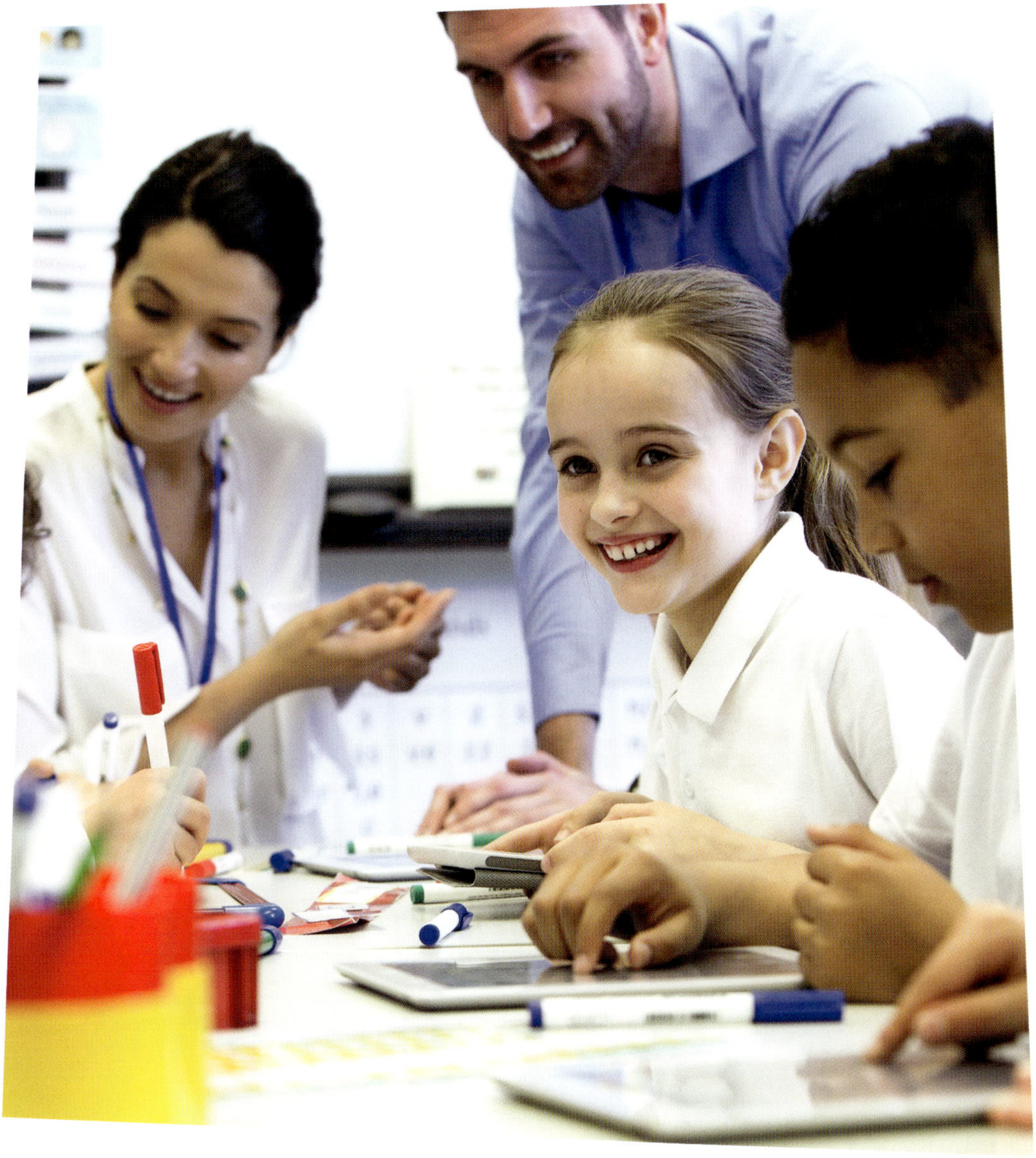

They plan many things. They plan **assemblies**. They plan fun events.

11

Principals work with teachers. They help teachers get ready for the school year.

13

They work with librarians.
They make sure the school
library has new books.

What is your favorite book?

Principals work with parents. They tell parents what is happening at the school.

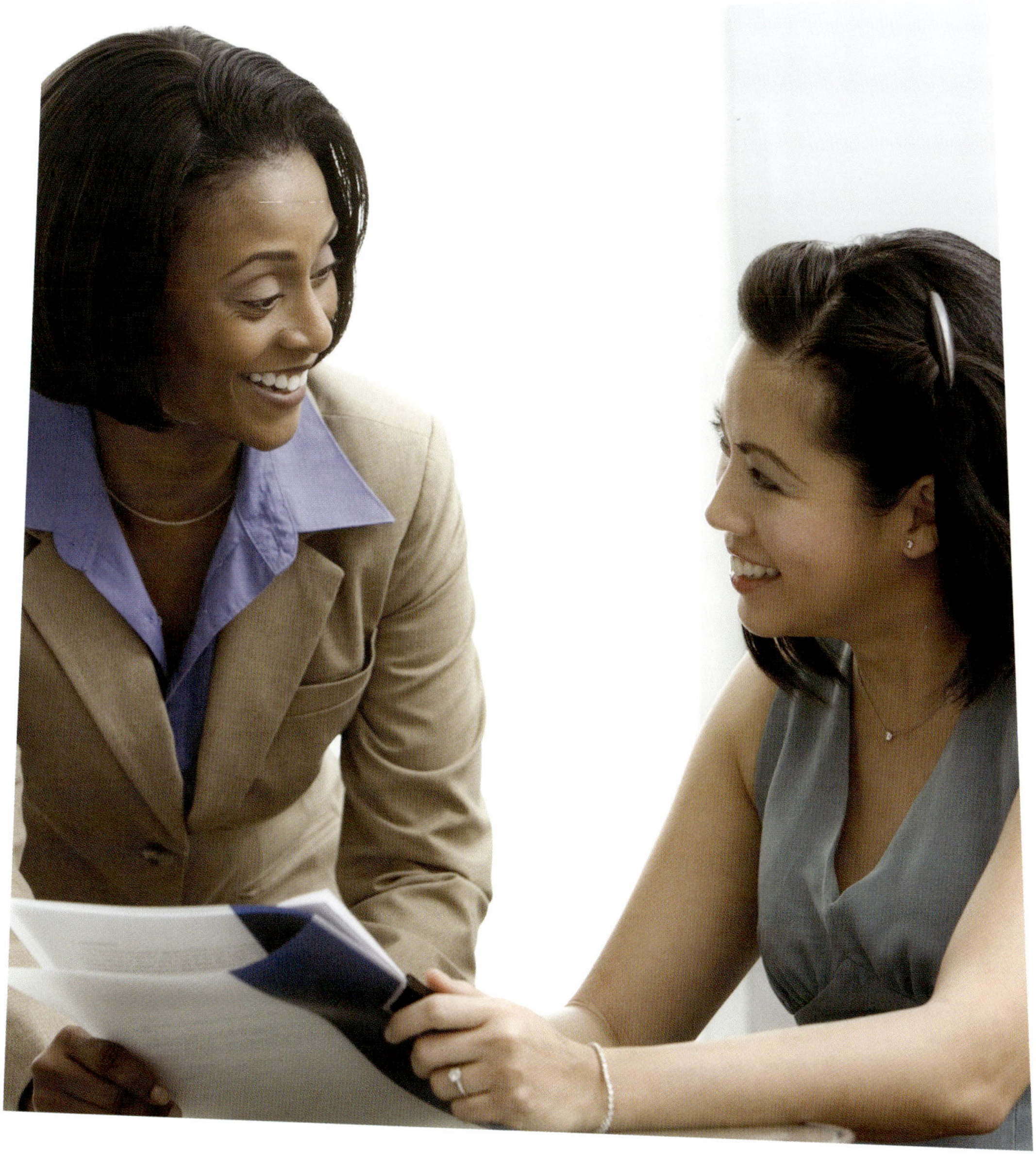

Some make rules. These help students do well. Teachers help students follow these rules.

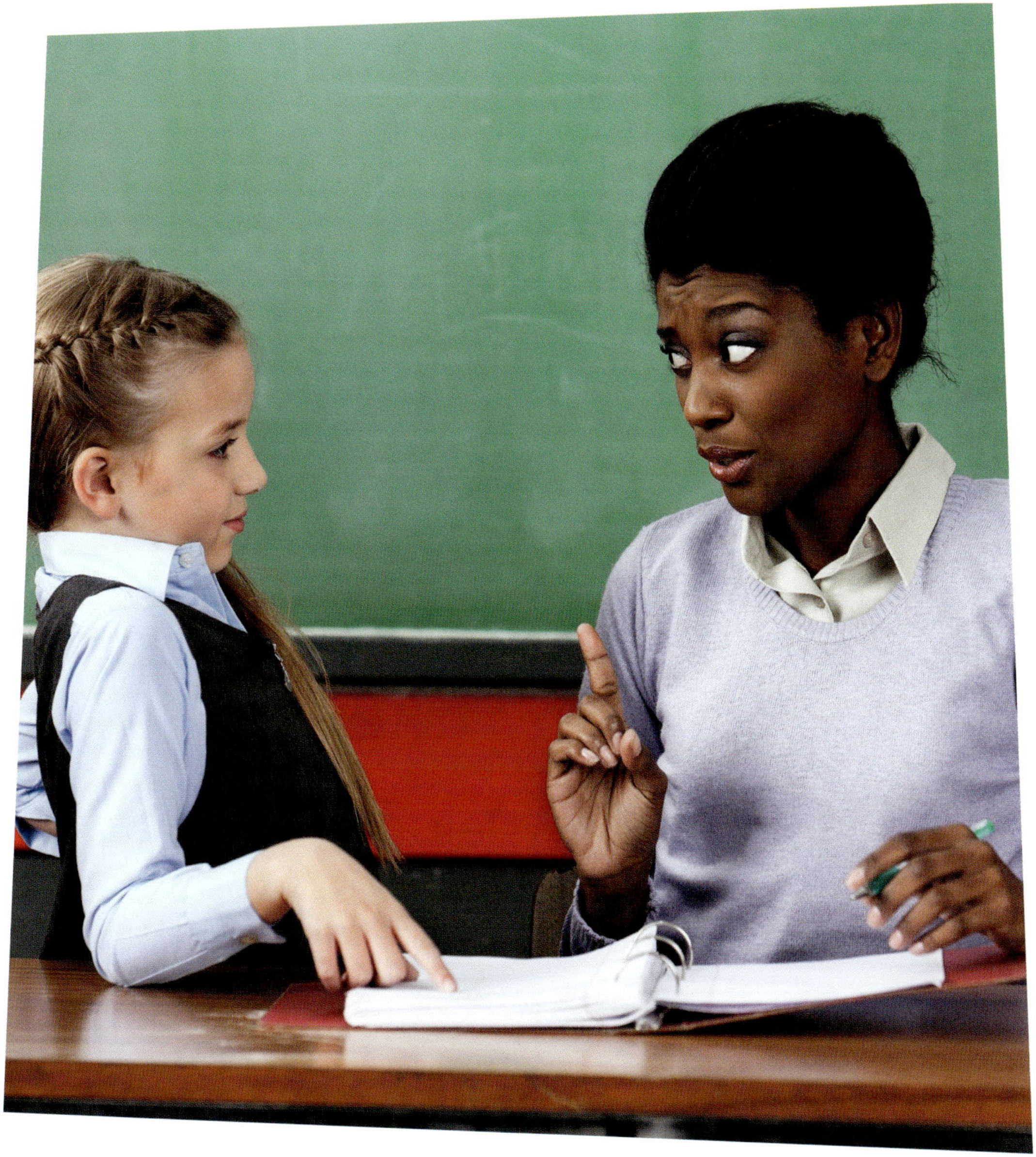

Principals start the day early. They come in before school starts. They prepare for the day. They work hard.

How do you prepare for the day?

Principals have **school pride**. They like going to school. They want students to like it, too.

What would you like to ask a principal?

glossary & index

glossary

assemblies (uh-SEM-bleez) meetings of students and teachers usually for learning or fun

improve (im-PROOV) to get better or to make better

school pride (SKOOL PRIDE) the feeling of excitement about your school and its accomplishments

index

assemblies, 10

improve, 6

lead, 6
librarians, 14

parents, 16
plan, 10

rules, 18

school clubs, 6
sports teams, 6
students, 8, 18, 22

teachers, 8, 12, 18